SWINGING FOR THE FENCES

LIFE IN THE NEGRO LEAGUES

A WHOLE NEW LEAGUE

WAYNE L. WILSON

PURPLE TOAD
PUBLISHING

PUBLISHER'S NOTE
This series, Swinging for the Fences: Life in the Negro Leagues, covers racism in United States history and how it affected professional baseball. Some of the events told in this series may be disturbing to young readers.

SWINGING FOR THE

FENCES

LIFE IN THE
NEGRO LEAGUES

A 4 VOL. SERIES

A Whole New League
by Wayne L. Wilson
Barnstorming
by Michael DeMocker
Legends of the Leagues
by Pete DiPrimio
Breaking the Barriers
by Russell Roberts

ABOUT THE AUTHOR
Wayne L. Wilson has authored numerous biographical and historical books for children and young adults. He received a Master of Arts in Education with a specialization in Sociology and Anthropology from UCLA. He is also a screenwriter and member of the Writer's Guild of America.

Publisher's Cataloging-in-Publication Data
Wilson, Wayne.
  A whole new league / written by Wayne Wilson.
    p. cm.
Includes bibliographic references, glossary, and index.
ISBN 9781624692789
1. Negro leagues—History—Juvenile literature. 2. Baseball—United States—History—Juvenile literature. I. Series: Swinging For The Fences : Life in the Negro Leagues.
  GV865.A1 2017
  796.357
Library of Congress Control Number: 2016937176
ebook ISBN: 9781624692796

TICKETS

Chapter One
A Legend Is Born   4
Baseball and Slavery   11

Chapter Two
A Pitching Sensation   12
The Gentlemen's Agreement   17

Chapter Three
A Born Leader   18
Crossing the Color Line   23

Chapter Four
It's Showtime   24
The Page Fence Giants   31

Chapter Five
A Whole New League   32

Timeline   40

Chapter Notes   42

Further Reading   44

Books   44

Works Consulted   44

On the Internet   45

Glossary   46

Index   48

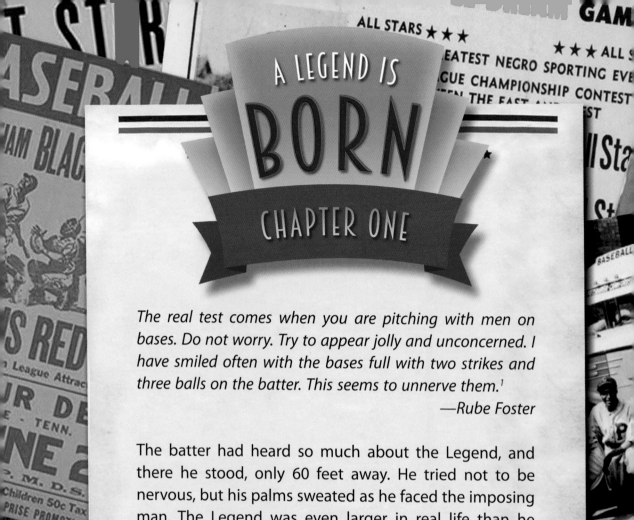

A LEGEND IS BORN

CHAPTER ONE

The real test comes when you are pitching with men on bases. Do not worry. Try to appear jolly and unconcerned. I have smiled often with the bases full with two strikes and three balls on the batter. This seems to unnerve them.[1]

—Rube Foster

The batter had heard so much about the Legend, and there he stood, only 60 feet away. He tried not to be nervous, but his palms sweated as he faced the imposing man. The Legend was even larger in real life than he thought. He was about 6 feet 2 inches tall and weighed at least 250 pounds. People talked about his pitching speed, and how he had a great curveball and a fastball that melted bats.

Today, the batter finally saw it for himself. The stories were true. The Legend threw the ball faster than anyone he'd ever seen in his life! All the players batting before him had failed to get a hit.

Called the Father of Negro Baseball, Andrew "Rube" Foster was one of the greatest pitchers and managers of his time. He organized the first black baseball league, the Negro National League.

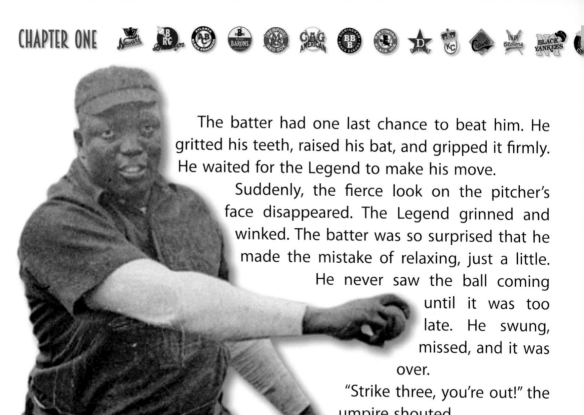

The batter had one last chance to beat him. He gritted his teeth, raised his bat, and gripped it firmly. He waited for the Legend to make his move.

Suddenly, the fierce look on the pitcher's face disappeared. The Legend grinned and winked. The batter was so surprised that he made the mistake of relaxing, just a little. He never saw the ball coming until it was too late. He swung, missed, and it was over.

"Strike three, you're out!" the umpire shouted.

The batter hated losing, but he smiled as he watched the big man casually walk off the mound and wave to his loudly cheering fans. The Legend, Mr. Andrew "Rube" Foster, had won another game. By the end of the 1903 season, he'd win an amazing 54 games.

Rube Foster is one of the giants of baseball history. Called "The Father of Black Baseball," he was not only one of the greatest pitchers and managers in the early twentieth century, he was also the founder of the Negro National League. It was the first successful baseball league for black

players. Foster was able to achieve this incredible feat despite facing racial prejudice throughout his life.

Andrew Foster was born on September 17, 1879, in Calvert, Texas. His father, Andrew Foster Sr., was the reverend of a church in the community. Andy went to his father's church every Sunday morning. Every Sunday afternoon, he went to the field to play baseball. In grade school he formed a neighborhood baseball team so that he could play baseball every day.[2]

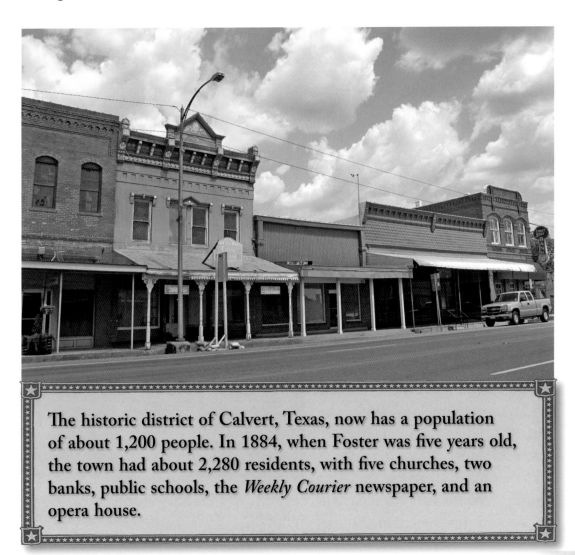

The historic district of Calvert, Texas, now has a population of about 1,200 people. In 1884, when Foster was five years old, the town had about 2,280 residents, with five churches, two banks, public schools, the *Weekly Courier* newspaper, and an opera house.

Andy's mother died when he was young. His father remarried and moved the family to southwestern Texas. Andy quit school after the eighth grade. He ran away from home to Fort Worth to try to make a living playing baseball.

In 1896, at the age of 17 and already over six-feet tall, Andrew was a pitcher for the Waco Yellow Jackets, an independent black baseball club. During their spring training, he pitched batting practice against some of the big-league clubs. The team traveled by freight train to many of their games. Foster once wrote that he and his teammates were often barred from going into other people's homes. At the time, some blacks considered baseball low class and not a very gentlemanly sport.[3]

Over the next few years, Andrew's reputation as a great pitcher began to build among black and white fans. When he was 21, Foster was invited to pitch against Connie Mack's Philadelphia Athletics in Hot Springs, Arkansas. This is where he earned his nickname, Rube.

Connie Mack was a Hall of Fame manager known for insisting his players be gentlemen.

He outpitched Rube Waddell, the top star of the all-white, pennant-winning Athletics. He left Hot Springs and headed north with fans calling him the "Rube beater." After awhile it was shortened to "Rube."[4]

Rube joined the Chicago Union Giants, the best Midwest team in black baseball, or "blackball." In his first appearance with the team he struggled as a pinch hitter, but this quickly changed when he took the mound as a pitcher. He lost only one game in three months with the team.[5]

Foster left the club and played for a short time with a white semipro ballclub at Otsego, Michigan. In Otsego he showed off his tremendous ability as a pitcher. He also developed one of his most famous pitches, the fadeaway, or screwball. The pitch came out of his right hand and broke like a hard curveball in reverse, into right-handed hitters, away from lefties, and paralyzing to all of them.[6]

Rube Waddell struck out more hitters than any pitcher of his time and led the majors in strikeouts for 6 straight years.

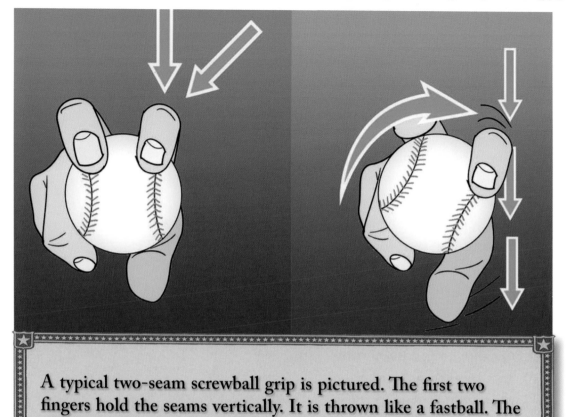

A typical two-seam screwball grip is pictured. The first two fingers hold the seams vertically. It is thrown like a fastball. The difference is turning the wrist counter-clockwise (if right-handed) as you throw.

After developing his killer screwball, along with a number of other pitches, Foster returned to blackball. In 1902, he began hurling for Frank Leland's Chicago Union Giants, one of the best black teams in the Midwest.

Foster had a reputation for changing teams, and he later jumped to the Cuban X-Giants in Philadelphia. (The players on this team were actually African Americans. They posed as Cubans to attract white fans.) He pitched for $40 a month, plus 15 cents per meal. He was badly beaten in his first game, but then got a new catcher and won the next 44. His final victory in 1902 came against the Philadelphia Giants, who had been the black champions in 1901.

Baseball and Slavery

The history of black baseball goes as far back as slavery in the South. Former slaves remembered playing baseball when they were young. They called the game "town ball." As one man remembered, "I never did dance, but I sure could play baseball and make home runs!" Black and white kids played baseball together on the plantation, but that changed as they got older.

The slaves often used makeshift balls and bats during games. In those days, no one said, "Let's get a team together." They said, "Let's get a nine together." If a ball was caught on the first bounce, it was called an out. During the earliest years of baseball, players did not have catcher's masks, gloves, chest guards, or batting helmets. A runner was out if the other team threw the ball at him and hit him.[1]

Union prisoners play a game of town ball during the Civil War, 1863.

"Rube had a way to grip that ball, throw underhand, and he could hum it. He was a trick pitcher, always tried to trick you into doing something wrong. If you were a big enough fool to listen to him, he'd have you looking at something else and strike you out!"

—Willie Powell, Negro League pitcher[1]

After so many victories, Foster's confidence grew. He declared himself "the best pitcher in the country," and most people agreed. His knowledge about pitching later became the gospel of the pitching arts. Many professional players followed his tips. He once stated: "The three great principles of pitching are good control, when to pitch certain balls, and where to pitch them. The longer you are in the game, the more you should gain by experience."[2]

Rube Foster made many players nervous by smiling before throwing pitches, and he often tricked batters into striking out.

Most of the white big-league managers and pitching coaches did not want to admit that Foster inspired or influenced them. Many managers would sneak him into their practices to teach their players how to play the game.

For example, John McGraw, the great manager of the New York Giants, asked Rube to teach his famous screwball to his pitching stars Christy Mathewson and Iron Man McGinnity. Mathewson's wins leaped from 14 in 1902 to 34 in 1903. McGinnity won over 30 games for the first time in his life, and the Giants jumped from last place to second.[3]

John McGraw and Christy Mathewson. Mathewson called his new pitch the fadeaway. With this pitch, he became the only pitcher to be in the top ten in both career wins and earned run average.

Many saw Mathewson as one of the greatest pitchers of his era. He and McGinnity became Hall of Famers. Mathewson said he learned his famous fadeaway pitch from Foster.[4]

Rube was highly respected by his fellow ballplayers. Frank Chance, a Hall of Fame first baseman for the Chicago Cubs, said this about Rube: "He is the most finished product I've ever seen in the pitcher's box!" Honus Wagner, a Hall of Fame shortstop for the Pittsburgh Pirates, called him "One of the greatest pitchers of all time."[5]

Many baseball scholars believe that Foster's strength and speed made his fastball almost unhittable. He weighed at least 260 pounds during his best years, and this helped to add to his legend as a giant. Even after a rare loss, the headline in a newspaper covering organized black baseball read: "Foster's Speed Frightens in Loss."[6]

Honus Wagner

In most cases, being on a team with Rube Foster was the path to success. Rube signed with the Cuban X-Giants in 1903, one of the top teams in blackball. He immediately became their ace pitcher. He won a remarkable 54 games, losing only one. In a bitterly fought playoff over the Philadelphia Giants, Foster won 4 games, leading the X-Giants to victory in the 1903 "Colored Championship of the World"—black baseball's World Series.[7]

The next year, Rube Foster, along with some of his teammates from the X-Giants, switched to the Philadelphia Giants. Just before the start of the World Series, Rube became sick. Players from the X-Giants claimed he wasn't sick and that he was just afraid to play them. Rube showed up for the first game, winning 9-4 with 18 strikeouts. The X-Giants won the second game,

The 1904 Philadelphia Giants, with Rube Foster (back, second from left)

but Rube triumphed in the final game of the playoffs, leading the team to a pennant.[8]

During the 1905 season, Foster won 51 of 55 games from major and minor teams and guided the Philadelphia Giants to two more championships (1905 and 1906), making them the best team of the era. Rube was in his prime as a pitcher, and Wagner once again paid him a compliment: "Foster is the smoothest pitcher I've ever seen." [9]

By this time, Rube had learned that being smart—pitching with your brains—is just as important as pitching with your arm. He once wrote an article on pitching in *Sol White's Baseball Guide*, which was published by his manager. In it he said that the real test of a pitcher comes when the bases are filled. When a batter is eager to hit the ball, he wrote, waste time pitching to him. And while the crowd is yelling for him to hit it, "waste a few balls and try his nerve; the majority of times you will win out by drawing him into hitting at a wide one."[10]

Foster would do anything for a win. Topsy Hartsel, of the major league's Philadelphia A's, had the edge on him with the tying and winning runs on base. The catcher called for Foster to pitch a walk. He threw a strike instead. The catcher called again for a walk. Foster threw another strike. While the crowd screamed and stomped their feet in the stands, Foster asked the umpire to make Hartsel get his feet in the box. The second Topsy looked down, "STRIKE THREE whistled over. Rube walked off the mound laughing."[11]

The Gentlemen's Agreement

In July 1887, the Newark Little Giants were facing the Chicago White Stockings in an exhibition game. The Little Giants had two black players: Fleet Walker as catcher and George Stovey as pitcher. Cap Anson, Chicago's star player, refused to play against them or any team that welcomed black players. Fearing a revolt by Anson and other white players, the league owners of the Board of the International League made a secret agreement. Called the "Gentlemen's Agreement," they promised to sign no more black players into the league. All black players, no matter how great, would be kept out of organized baseball. The ban would last for the next 60 years.[1]

The 1887 Chicago White Stockings, with Cap Anson in the center. Anson led the movement that resulted in the creation of the "Gentlemen's Agreement."

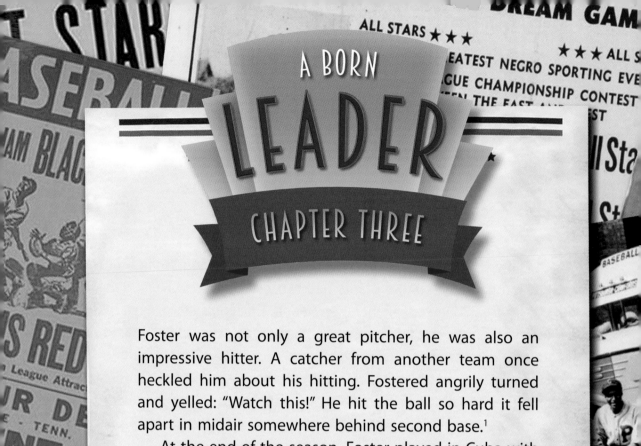

A BORN LEADER

CHAPTER THREE

Foster was not only a great pitcher, he was also an impressive hitter. A catcher from another team once heckled him about his hitting. Fostered angrily turned and yelled: "Watch this!" He hit the ball so hard it fell apart in midair somewhere behind second base.[1]

At the end of the season, Foster played in Cuba with the Fe ballclub. He led the league with 9 victories. His leadership skills shone as he took charge of the team and pitched half of their games.

Already known as one of the greatest baseball players of the 1900s, Foster could have retired right then. He didn't want to. He wanted to do more than just perform on the baseball field.

After returning to the United States, he asked the Philadelphia Giants for a bigger salary. When they refused to pay him more, he walked off the team. In 1906, he accepted an offer from his old boss, Frank

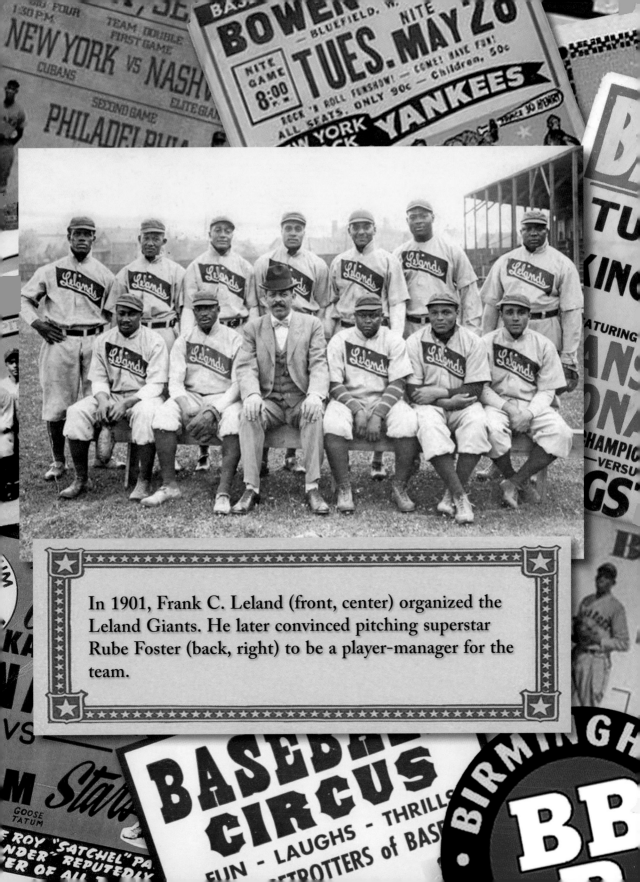

In 1901, Frank C. Leland (front, center) organized the Leland Giants. He later convinced pitching superstar Rube Foster (back, right) to be a player-manager for the team.

Leland, to be manager of the Leland Giants in Chicago. He brought with him players from the Philadelphia Giants and other teams.

Foster starred on the Leland Giants for three seasons as a player and field manager. He turned the Giants into the masters of the "raceball," meaning the team was always moving, always on the go. Everyone ran, breaking from first on nearly every pitch. Foster would have his players bunt, steal, and use hit-and-run tactics that would drive pitchers crazy. This racehorse style of play made pitchers nervous, because a player could go from first to third without the ball ever being hit beyond the pitcher's mound.

Frank Leland

Rube Foster, the "hurler" from Texas in 1907, led the team to 110 victories (48 in a row) and a Chicago City League Pennant. In 1908, the Leland Giants rode in a private Pullman car to Hot Springs, Arkansas, for spring training. They were the first black team to take the train in such style.

Another big event happened for Rube in 1908. He married Sarah Watts. They would have two children.

Foster continued to throw his feared screwball. His pitching, along with his creative plays and strategies, helped the Giants win 123 games out of 129 in 1910. Foster later split with Frank Leland and decided to build his own team. He brought players from both the Leland Giants and the Philadelphia Giants. His new club was loaded with some of the best baseball talent of the time.

The team was called the Chicago American Giants. Foster later called it the greatest team he ever assembled, with stars such as John Henry "Pop" Lloyd, Pete Hill, Grant "Home Run" Johnson, Frank Wickware, and Pat Dougherty. Foster managed and pitched for the team, driving them to a remarkable 128-6 season record. Even though he was past his prime, Rube still added a 13-2 record as a pitcher for the team.[2]

One of Foster's prized catchers was future Hall of Famer Pop Lloyd. Pop became known for scooping up a gloveful of dirt from the ground every time he fielded the ball. Lean and lanky, he started his career as a catcher. His face was smashed so often by foul tips that he made a catcher's mask out of a wire basket.

Another great discovery was when the American Giants traveled to Fort Worth, Texas, for spring training. Thousands of people showed up to greet the team. The fans came in wagons, carriages, and streetcars. Rube spotted a man who was half Comanche and half African American throwing fastballs with unbelievable speed. Impressed, Rube joked, "Slow down there." The man turned to Rube and said, "If I really throw hard, you won't see it at all." Rube asked him his name. "Just call me

Pop Lloyd is said to be the greatest shortstop in Negro League history. He played for 27 years and had a lifetime batting average of .343. In Cuba he was called "The Shovel" for his great defense.

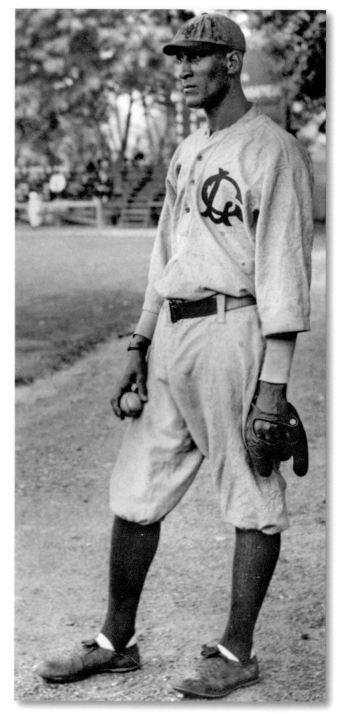

Cyclone." The name stuck, and Cyclone Joe Williams would one day join the Hall of Fame.[3]

With such a great lineup, the American Giants proudly promoted their upcoming games. Fans could attend the Giants games at the bargain price of only 50 cents for a box seat, with free ice water! On one Sunday the popular Giants drew over 11,000 people, "more than both the major league White Sox and Cubs teams on that same day." As Jim Bowman of the *Chicago Tribune* wrote, "Foster became the best known black man in Chicago."[4]

Cyclone Joe Williams was also known as Smokey Joe. In exhibition games against white major leaguers, he had a 20-7 record. He beat pitchers like Grover Cleveland Alexander and Walter Johnson. Williams was elected into the Hall of Fame in 1999.

Crossing the Color Line

1885 Keokuk, Iowa team with Bud Fowler (back, center)

The poor fellow's skin is against him. With his splendid abilities he would long ago have been on some good club had his color been white instead of black.

> —*Sporting Life,* about Bud Fowler, December 30, 1885[1]

Although he had many firsts, Jackie Robinson was not the first black player to compete in the minor leagues. That honor goes to second baseman John "Bud" Fowler. He played for the Massachusetts Live Oaks of the International Association in 1878. Fowler invented shin guards, which he fashioned out of wood.[2]

Moses Fleetwood Walker was born at a way station on the Underground Railroad for slaves escaping to Canada. The son of a doctor, he attended Oberlin College and played on the school baseball team as a catcher. In 1884, "Fleet" became the first black player to play in the major leagues. He played 42 games as a catcher with the Toledo Blue Stockings of the American Association.[3]

Moses Fleetwood Walker

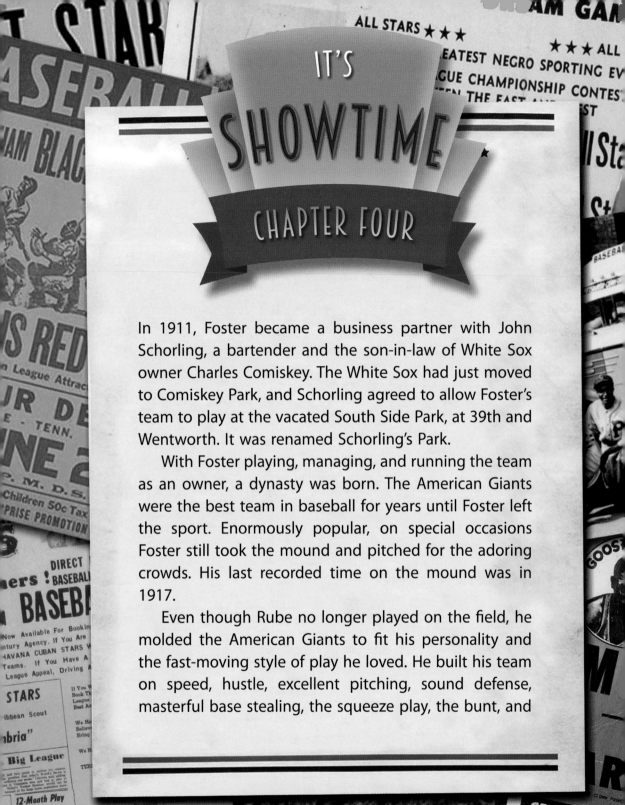

In 1911, Foster became a business partner with John Schorling, a bartender and the son-in-law of White Sox owner Charles Comiskey. The White Sox had just moved to Comiskey Park, and Schorling agreed to allow Foster's team to play at the vacated South Side Park, at 39th and Wentworth. It was renamed Schorling's Park.

With Foster playing, managing, and running the team as an owner, a dynasty was born. The American Giants were the best team in baseball for years until Foster left the sport. Enormously popular, on special occasions Foster still took the mound and pitched for the adoring crowds. His last recorded time on the mound was in 1917.

Even though Rube no longer played on the field, he molded the American Giants to fit his personality and the fast-moving style of play he loved. He built his team on speed, hustle, excellent pitching, sound defense, masterful base stealing, the squeeze play, the bunt, and

The American Giants featured some of the biggest stars in Negro baseball. Rube considered the team to be "the greatest baseball talent ever assembled."

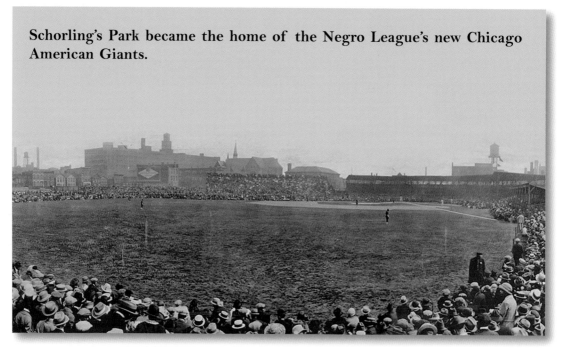

Schorling's Park became the home of the Negro League's new Chicago American Giants.

the hit-and-run. If you could not bunt the ball, you could not play for Rube Foster. He fined any member of his championship team five dollars if they were tagged standing up. "You're supposed to slide," he'd snap. He often signaled plays with his pipe.[1]

Foster was tough. He carried a revolver with him wherever he went. But he also could be gentle and kind. His habit was to call friends and strangers "darling." He was loved by his players, and he'd take money out of his own pockets to help pay their wages. When asked if given the chance how his teams would do against the white big-leaguers, Foster calmly said, "If we play the best clubs in the land, white clubs as you say, it will be a case of Greek meeting Greek. I fear *nobody!*"[2]

This wasn't just talk. Rube had experience against some of their best players.

Even though the game was segregated, the top black teams played against the white major league teams in the off-season. These "barnstorming" events helped the players earn extra income. They also gave the teams a chance to prove their skills on an equal playing field. Foster did great in these matchups against legendary pitchers, such as Cy Young and Mordecai Brown.

Many of the white big league teams avoided playing teams with Rube Foster and other great black players. Ty Cobb was one of the greatest players in the major leagues, but he was also known for his extremely racist views. When his Detroit Tigers toured Cuba after their pennant-winning season, he stayed home rather than face the black players.

The next year his teammates convinced him to play. He was outhit and outplayed by Pop Lloyd, Home Run Johnson, and Bruce Petway. Ty Cobb was so humiliated that he vowed never to play against another all-black team.

Other white players went to Cuba because they wanted to. They not only played on the same field as black players, they also lived with black players in the same building. Sometimes white players who needed extra money would play on black professional teams in cities, such as Chicago. To

Ty Cobb was not used to being outplayed. He won 9 consecutive batting titles.

protect their jobs, they would use fake names and pull their hat bills down over their faces so that they would not be recognized.

The American Giants won championships from 1910 through 1922, every year except 1916. As a player and manager, Foster had an outstanding career. He was able to give baseball even more, though, as an owner. He excelled as a negotiator with the white men who controlled teams and venues. He often secured for his black players more than half of the game's proceeds for appearances against white teams. Before Foster got involved in the business end, black baseball was scattered and unorganized. Many of the attempts to start a black league had failed.

After the Civil War, there was still a lot of racial tension, especially in the South. Many black people began moving from the South to the North to

DUNCAN   C.BELL   MOTHELL   McCALL   DRAKE   SWEATT   WILKINSON   DR. SMITH   SPEDDEN   POMPEZ   FOSTER   BOLDEN   SANTOP

Rube Foster at the October 11, 1924, opening game of the Negro World Series. It was the first meeting between teams that were officially

escape the racial turmoil. In the early 1900s, factory jobs became available in the North. Many more black people moved north for better jobs. They became a major part of the labor force in the larger cities, such as Chicago—but whites still owned the factories and the profits. The black population remained in poverty. Conditions were better than in the South, but the North also had its racial issues. By 1919, a violent race riot broke out in Chicago.

Meanwhile, black athletes were still barred from playing in white leagues. Black clubs depended on white stadium owners for a place to play ball.

The great novelist Ralph Ellison has written that even though blacks have experienced racism in all areas of society, even baseball, they have still been able to turn it into something positive, something in which they can

recognized as league champions. In this series, the National League Kansas City Monarchs defeated the Eastern Colored League Hilldale 5-4, with one tie game.

Born in Oklahoma City in 1914, Ralph Ellison was an American novelist and scholar. He is best known for his award-winning novel *Invisible Man*, which received the National Book Award in 1953.

joyfully participate. Many black sportswriters, like Ellison, saw baseball as more than just a game. They viewed it as a "source of interest, pride, and race glory."[3]

Black fans had also been hit with the "baseball madness" that gripped the rest of the country. They enjoyed watching teams like the Cubans and the American Giants. Blackball was seen as a huge step toward social change.

Charles Starkes, sports editor of the *Kansas City Call*, wrote: "Here in Kansas City we see baseball as a wonderful contributor to the solution of an ancient race problem."[4]

But would there be a future for black baseball?

The Page Fence Giants

Bud Fowler and Homerun Johnson partnered with the Page Woven Wire Fence Company to form the Page Fence Giants. They played against major league teams like the Cincinnati Reds. To drum up ticket sales, this barnstorming team rode into town in a Pullman railroad car. Before each game, they paraded through the area in uniform on bicycles. Their showmanship and gifted athleticism drew huge crowds.

On game day, souvenirs were handed out with a picture of the Giants on one side and a picture of the Page Woven Wire Fence Company on the other. It was a promotional success. The Page Fence Giants were considered one of the best teams in African American baseball history.[1]

The Page Fence Giants

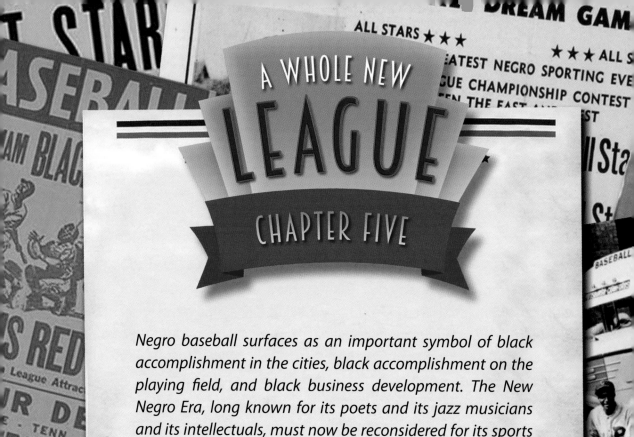

A WHOLE NEW LEAGUE

CHAPTER FIVE

Negro baseball surfaces as an important symbol of black accomplishment in the cities, black accomplishment on the playing field, and black business development. The New Negro Era, long known for its poets and its jazz musicians and its intellectuals, must now be reconsidered for its sports figures.[1]

—Clement Price (Historian)

Rube Foster understood the need for change. He wanted to prove that black and white ballplayers were equal. In the winter of 1919, he made a huge decision. He called together the owners of the best black clubs in the Midwest. These businessmen would establish a Negro National League (NNL). The owners met in a Kansas City YMCA on Friday, February 13, 1920, to hammer out an agreement. At first, Foster wanted it to be a completely

The 1922 annual meeting of the Negro National League.
Two years earlier, under the guidance of Rube Foster
(front, center), team owners met at the YMCA in
Kansas City, and created the Negro National League.
Foster was named president and treasurer.

Rube Foster as manager of the Chicago American Giants

black league, but he was willing to admit one white owner: J.L. Wilkinson of Kansas City.

The league was modeled after Major League Baseball. Foster wanted to bring black clubs from the east and west under one organization. He hoped that the black and white champs of each league would play each other in a real World Series.

Foster overcame many obstacles to organize the NNL. The first teams were Chicago, Indianapolis, Detroit, Birmingham, Memphis, Kansas City, St. Louis, and Cleveland. Foster served as the first president and treasurer of the league. He also continued to serve as manager and owner of the Chicago American Giants. Once the league officially started play, Foster's team rewarded him by winning the first three pennants.

Foster's league motto was "We are the ship, all else is the sea."[2] With Foster as captain of the ship, it remained afloat for ten golden years. A well-respected leader, he turned black baseball into a successful business. He was completely devoted to the league's success. He would even help teams that were in financial trouble. Players' salaries rose to the highest

levels, and players received regular bonuses. Foster worked tirelessly to make the league and its teams a major success. He even gave up Oscar Charleston, who was praised as the "best black player of all time," to the Indianapolis ABCs in order to strengthen that team.

The press praised the league as a great advancement for the black race. As Foster explained, his goal was "to create a profession that would equal the earning capacity of any other profession . . . keep Colored baseball from the control of whites, and do something concrete for the loyalty of the race."[3]

By 1923, his league had become a runaway success. *The Chicago Defender* reported, "Four hundred thousand black fans turned out that season to see Foster's teams play, and his men rode in comfort from town to town aboard specially hired Pullman cars."[4]

Only the most popular teams were able to ride major-league style in luxurious Pullman cars.

Foster was extremely proud of his American Giants. He wrote in 1924: "They have done wonders. When there were no other clubs in existence the Giants traveled thousands of miles to play ball. The Giants have done more to keep a friendly feeling between the Negroes and whites than any other institution of its kind in the world."[5]

Foster's new league enjoyed popularity at home and abroad. His clubs played exhibition games as far away as Japan. Teams such as the Chicago American Giants and Kansas City Monarchs often sold more tickets than

Teams such as the 1934 Kansas City Monarchs often brought in more money than the white baseball teams. They opened the door for black baseball leagues in the south and east. Foster laid the groundwork for the future success of the league.

The St. Louis Giants changed their name to the St. Louis Stars after joining the NNL. The Stars won three pennants in the four years from 1928 to 1931.

their white counterparts. The success of the league inspired other black leagues to form in the south and east.

Foster put in long days and traveled far and wide while managing the NNL. Eventually his busy schedule affected his health. In 1925 he was exposed to a gas leak in his home and fainted. He was revived, but he never fully recovered. His condition grew worse, and he was moved to a hospital in 1926.

Foster never saw his team win the pennant and the World Series in 1926 and 1927. He died of a heart attack on December 9, 1930, while still in the hospital.

The NNL had suffered from his long absence. The Great Depression also brought financial hardships to the league. Without Foster's vision and hard work, the league dissolved in 1931. The decade fondly called "The Golden Age" was over.[6]

Dave Malarcher was called the best third basemen in black baseball. He developed into a brilliant baseball strategist and took over as manager after Rube became ill.

At Foster's funeral, more than 3,000 mourners stood outside the church in the falling snow. The casket was carried out to the hymn "Rock of Ages." Dave Malarcher, who was a third baseman for the American Giants, had this to say about Rube choosing to come back to play in the Negro leagues when he could have kept playing white semi-pro ball. "Rube refused to go," Malarcher explained, "because he knew all we had to do was keep developing Negro League baseball, keep it up to a high standard and the time would come when the white leagues would have to admit us, and when the time did come we would be able to measure up."[7]

Foster's efforts paved the way for other black athletes. An article in the *Pittsburgh Courier* stated: "Rube Foster tried to get black baseball respectability. Otherwise this reservoir of black talent, which is the backbone of the major leagues today, might not have been there. . . . This pasture, this harvest, this crop was the result of Rube Foster's enterprise."[8]

The Father of Black Baseball died, but his vision of a league in which black players were respected had been achieved. Andrew Rube Foster's accomplishments were finally recognized. He was inducted into the Baseball Hall of Fame in 1981.

Opposite: Memorial plaque for Rube Foster

ANDREW (RUBE) FOSTER

RATED FOREMOST MANAGER AND EXECUTIVE IN
HISTORY OF NEGRO LEAGUES. ACCLAIMED TOP
PITCHER IN BLACK BASEBALL FOR NEARLY A
DECADE IN EARLY 1900s. FORMED CHICAGO
AMERICAN GIANTS IN 1911 AND BUILT THEM
INTO MIDWEST'S DOMINANT BLACK TEAM. IN
1920 HE ORGANIZED NEGRO NATIONAL LEAGUE.
HEADED LEAGUE AND MANAGED CHICAGO TEAM
UNTIL RETIREMENT FOLLOWING 1926 SEASON.

1866	The National League plays its first game.
1879	Andrew Rube Foster is born on September 17. Thomas Edison invents the lightbulb.
1880	Lee Richmond pitches a perfect game.
1883	The Brooklyn Bridge opens.
1884	Moses Fleetwood Walker becomes the first African American player in Major League Baseball.
1885	The first black professional baseball team is formed in Long Island by waiters of the Argyle Hotel—the Cuban Giants.
1887	International League owners make a Gentlemen's Agreement to sign no new contracts with black baseball players. The National Colored Baseball League is started, but it folds after two weeks.
1891	Sir Arthur Conan Doyle writes *The Adventures of Sherlock Holmes*. James Naismith invents basketball.
1894	The Pullman railroad strike cripples railroad traffic nationwide and underscores the need for workers' unions.
1896	With its decision on *Plessy v. Ferguson*, the U.S. Supreme Court begins 60 years of "separate but equal" segregation.
1899	William E. B. DuBois becomes the first black person to earn a Ph.D. from Harvard.
1900	The American League is established
1901	U.S. President William McKinley is assassinated. Rough Rider Theodore Roosevelt becomes president.
1902	Immigration in the U.S. reaches a record high.
1903	Major League Baseball is formed. The first World Series is played. The Wright Brothers make the first flight at Kitty Hawk.
1904	Alta Weiss becomes the first woman to play professional baseball.
1905	The first U.S. movie theater opens.
1908	The song "Take Me Out to the Ballgame" is written. Jack Johnson becomes the first black heavyweight champion.
1909	The National Association for the Advancement of Colored People (NAACP) is founded.
1910	Rube Foster forms the Chicago American Giants. Boy Scouts of America is chartered.
1912	The HMS *Titanic* sinks. Oreo cookies are introduced. Parachutes are invented.
1913	The Apollo Theater is built in Harlem, New York. Henry Ford creates the first moving assembly line.
1914	World War I begins. Mother's Day is created.
1916	Jeanette Rankin becomes the first Congresswoman. Tanks are new in warfare.
1917	African American businesswoman Madam C.J. Walker (Sarah Breedlove) becomes the first self-made female millionaire. The U.S. enters World War I.

1918 World War I ends. "The Star-Spangled Banner" is sung at a baseball game for the first time.

1919 Eight members of the Chicago White Socks are banned for life in the "Black Sox Scandal" that took place during the World Series.

1920 Rube Foster organizes a meeting at the Kansas City YMCA and forms the Negro National League. The 19th Amendment is ratified, giving women the right to vote.

1921 Baseball is heard for the first time over the radio.

1922 The National Football League (NFL) is formed. Insulin is discovered. Known for his great foot speed, James "Cool Papa" Bell joins the St. Louis Stars as a pitcher.

1923 The Eastern Colored League is established.

1924 The Kansas City Monarchs win the first Negro League World Series. Citizenship is granted to all Native Americans.

1925 The Jazz Age begins. Lou Gehrig begins his career as a first baseman for the New York Yankees.

1926 The future giants of jazz, John Coltrane and Miles Davis, are born. Magician Harry Houdini dies. Rube Foster suffers a nervous breakdown and is committed to a hospital.

1927 *The Jazz Singer*, the first major film with sound, is released. Duke Ellington makes a name for himself at the Cotton Club in Harlem. Charles Lindbergh flies alone nonstop across the Atlantic in 33 hours.

1928 The first Mickey Mouse cartoon debuts. Penicillin is discovered. Sliced bread is invented. The record-breaking outfielder Ty Cobb retires.

1929 The stock market crash leads to the Great Depression. Babe Ruth hits his 500th home run. Martin Luther King Jr. is born.

1930 Andrew Rube Foster dies.

1931 The National Negro League dissolves.

1933 A new Negro National League is formed. Organized by Pittsburgh bar owner Gus Green, it starts with seven teams.

1937 The Negro American League is formed.

1946 Jackie Robinson signs with the Brooklyn Dodgers.

1947 Jackie Robinson becomes the first black player in Major League Baseball in the modern era.

The Cleveland Indians sign the first black player to play in the American League, Larry Doby.

1952 More than 150 former Negro League players have joined the Major League Baseball system, either in the major or minor leagues.

Chapter One: A Legend Is Born

1. Mark Ribowsky, *A Complete History of the Negro Leagues: 1884 to 1955* (New York: A Birch Lane Press Book, 1995), p. 61.

2. Rube Foster, *Black History Now*, August 3, 2010, http://blackhistorynow.com/rube-foster/

3. John B. Holway, *Blackball Stars: Negro League Pioneers* (Westport, CT: Meckler Books, 1988), p. 9.

4. Ribowsky, pp. 54–55.

5. Andrew "Rube" Foster, Negro Leagues Baseball Museum, http://coe.k-state.edu/annex/nlbemuseum/history/players/fostera.html

6. Holway, p. 11.

FYI: Baseball and Slavery

1. Lawrence D. Hogan, *Shades of Glory: The Negro Leagues and the Story of African-American Baseball* (Washington, D.C.: National Geographic, 2006), pp. 5–6.

Chapter Two: A Pitching Sensation

1. John B. Holway, *Blackball Stars: Negro League Pioneers* (Westport, CT: Meckler Books, 1988), p. 14.

2. Mark Ribowsky, *A Complete History of the Negro Leagues: 1884 to 1955* (New York: A Birch Lane Press Book, 1995), p. 62.

3. Holway, p. 11.

4. Jordan French, *The Life and Legacy of Andrew "Rube" Foster: Baseball's Forgotten Legend*, http://www.nhd.org/wp-content/uploads/French_Junior.pdf

5. Timothy Odzer, "Rube Foster," Society for American Baseball Research, http://sabr.org/bioproj/person/fcf322f7

6. French.

7. Rube Foster, National Baseball Hall of Fame, http://baseballhall.org/hof/foster-rube

8. Holway, p. 12.

9. Andrew "Rube" Foster, Negro Leagues Baseball Museum, http://coe.k-state.edu/annex/nlbemuseum/history/players/fostera.html

10. Holway, p. 12.

11. John B. Holway, *The Complete Book of Baseball's Negro Leagues: The Other Half of Baseball History* (Fern Park, FL: Hastings House Publishers, 2001), p. 49.

FYI: The Gentlemen's Agreement

1. Artemus Ward, *Negro League Baseball*, "Baseball Discrimination," Dept. of Political Science, Northern Illinois University, http://www.niu.edu/polisci/faculty/profiles/ward/ward_files/NegroLeagueBaseball.ppt

Chapter Three: A Born Leader

1. John B. Holway, *Blackball Stars: Negro League Pioneers* (Westport, CT: Meckler Books, 1988), pp. 12–13.

2. Andrew "Rube" Foster, Negro Leagues Baseball Museum, http://coe.k-state.edu/annex/nlbemuseum/history/players/fostera.html

3. John B. Holway, *The Complete Book of Baseball's Negro Leagues: The Other Half of Baseball History* (Fern Park, FL: Hastings House Publishers, 2001), p. 74.

4. Holway, *Blackball Stars*, p. 16.

FYI: Crossing the Color Line

1. Mark Ribowsky, *A Complete History of the Negro Leagues: 1884 to 1955* (New York: A Birch Lane Press Book, 1995), p. 10.

2. Benjamin Hill, "Fowler: A 19th-Century Baseball Pioneer," http://www.milb.com/gen/articles/printer_friendly/milb/y2006/m02/d08/c41022.jsp

3. Moses "Fleet" Walker, Negro Leagues Baseball Museum, http://coe.k-state.edu/annex/nlbemuseum/history/players/walker.html

Chapter Four: It's Showtime

1. Andrew "Rube" Foster, Negro Leagues Baseball Museum, http://coe.k-state.edu/annex/nlbemuseum/history/players/fostera.html

2. Geoffrey C. Ward and Ken Burns, *Baseball: An Illustrated History* (New York: Alfred A. Knopf, Inc., 1994), p. 157.

3. Lawrence D. Hogan, *Shades of Glory: The Negro Leagues and the Story of African-American Baseball* (Washington, D.C.: National Geographic, 2006), p. 156.

4. Ibid., p. 157.

FYI: The Page Fence Giants

1. Hogan, Shades of Glory, pp. 73-77.

Chapter Five: A Whole New League

1. Lawrence D. Hogan, *Shades of Glory: The Negro Leagues and the Story of African-American Baseball* (Washington, D.C.: National Geographic, 2006), p. 156.

2. Chris Lamberti, "South Side Baseball Legend: Rube Foster." *Chicago Now,* March 28, 2012, http://www.chicagonow.com/white-sox-observer/2012/03/south-side-baseball-legend-rube-foster/

3. Geoffrey C. Ward and Ken Burns, *Baseball: An Illustrated History* (New York: Alfred A. Knopf, Inc., 1994), p. 158.

4. Ibid., p.157.

5. Lamberti.

6. Rube Foster, *Black History Now*, August 3, 2010, http://blackhistorynow.com/rube-foster/

7. William C. Rhoden, *Forty Million Dollar Slaves; The Rise, Fall, and Redemption of the Black Athlete* (New York: Three Rivers Press, 2010), p. 106.

8. John B. Holway, *The Complete Book of Baseball's Negro Leagues: The Other Half of Baseball History* (Fern Park, FL: Hastings House Publishers, 2001), pp. 271–272.

Books

Dixon, Phil, S. *Andrew "Rube" Foster: A Harvest On Freedom's Fields.* Xlibris Corporation, 2010.

Gay, Timothy M. *Satch, Dizzy & Rapid Robert: The Wild Saga of Interracial Baseball Before Jackie Robinson.* New York: Simon & Schuster, 2010.

Luke, Bob. *The Most Famous Woman In Baseball: Effa Manley and the Negro Leagues.* Washington, D.C.: Potomac Books, Inc., 2011.

Smolka, Bo. *The Story of the Negro Leagues.* Minneapolis: ABDO Publishing Company, 2013.

White, Sol. *Sol White's Official Baseball Guide.* South Orange, NJ: Summer Game Books, 2014.

Works Consulted

Hogan, Lawrence D. *Shades of Glory: The Negro Leagues and the Story of African-American Baseball.* Washington, D.C.: National Geographic, 2006.

Holway, John B. *Blackball Stars: Negro League Pioneers.* Westport, CT: Meckler Books, 1988.

Holway, John B. *The Complete Book of Baseball's Negro Leagues: The Other Half of Baseball History.* Fern Park, FL: Hastings House Publishers, 2001.

Lamberti, Chris. "South Side Baseball Legend: Rube Foster." *Chicago Now,* March 28, 2012. http://www.chicagonow.com/white-sox-observer/2012/03/south-side-baseball-legend-rube-foster/

McNeil, William F. *The California Winter League: America's First Integrated Professional Baseball League.* Jefferson, North Carolina: McFarland & Company, Inc., 2002.

Rhoden, William C. *Forty Million Dollar Slaves; The Rise, Fall, and Redemption of the Black Athlete,* New York: Three Rivers Press, 2010.

Ribowsky, Mark. *A Complete History of The Negro Leagues: 1884 to 1955.* New York: A Birch Lane Press Book, 1995.

Ward, Geoffrey C., and Ken Burns. *Baseball: An Illustrated History.* New York: Alfred A. Knopf, Inc., 1994.

On the Internet

Benjamin Hill, "Fowler: A 19th-Century Baseball Pioneer."
    http://www.milb.com/gen/articles/printer_friendly/milb/y2006/m02/
    d08/c41022.jsp

George Kirsch, "Blacks, Baseball and the Civil War."
    http://opinionator.blogs.nytimes.com/2014/09/23/blacks-baseball-
    and-the-civil-war/?_r=0

Moses "Fleet" Walker, Negro Leagues Baseball Museum.
    http://coe.k-state.edu/annex/nlbemuseum/history/players/walker.html

Negro Baseball Leagues.
    http://www.blackpast.org/aah/negro-baseball-leagues-1920-1950

"Only The Ball Was White" (Documentary about Negro Baseball League).
    http://mediaburn.org/video/only-the-ball-was-white-2/

Timothy Odzer, Rube Foster, Society for American Baseball Research.
    http://sabr.org/bioproj/person/fcf322f7

discrimination (dih-skrih-mih-NAY-shun)—Unfairly treating a person or a group of people differently from another person or group.

era (AYR-uh)—A period of time in history marked by a certain event or ruler.

Great Depression (GRAYT dee-PREH-shun)—A major breakdown in the U.S. economy that lasted from 1929 to 1940.

groundbreaking (GROUND-bray-king)—New ideas or methods that change the way things were always done.

heckle (HEK-ul)—To interrupt a speaker or performer with negative comments (to boo them).

legend (LEH-jund)—A story or collection of stories about a person who is known for doing something extremely well.

motto (MAH-toh)—A sentence, phrase, or word expressing the spirit or behavior of a person or organization.

negotiator (neh-GOH-she-ay-tor)—A person who deals or bargains to try to reach an agreement.

obstacle (OB-stuh-kul)—Something that gets in the way or makes a goal difficult to reach.

pennant (PEH-nunt)—In baseball, the prize that is awarded to the champions of the American or National league each year.

principle (PRIN-sih-pul)—A fundamental truth that serves as the foundation of a system of beliefs or behavior.

proceeds (PROH-seeds)—Money gained from an event or activity.

proposal (proh-POH-zul)—A detailed idea.

racism (RAY-sism)—A belief that people who look or act like oneself are better than others, and that it is okay to be mean to those others.

turmoil (TUR-moyl)—A state of great commotion or confusion.

PHOTO CREDITS: Pp. 7, 8, 11, 15, 27, 28, 35—Loc.gov. All other photos—Public Domain. Every measure has been taken to find all copyright holders of material used in this book. In the event any mistakes or omissions have happened within, attempts to correct them will be made in future editions of the book.

Alexander, Grover Cleveland   22
American Association   23
Anson, Cap   17
Baseball Hall of Fame   8, 15, 21, 22, 38
Bowman, Jim   22
Brown, Mordecai   27
Chance, Frank   15
Charleston, Oscar   35
Chicago American Giants   20, 22, 28, 34, 36, 38
Chicago Cubs   15, 22
Chicago Union Giants   9
Chicago White Stockings   17
Civil War   11, 29
Cobb, Ty   27
Colored Championship of the World   15
Comiskey, Charles   24
Connie Mack's Philadelphia Athletics   8
Cuban Fe   18
Cuban Giants   10, 15, 30, 40
Cuban X-Giants   10, 15
Detroit Tigers   27
Dougherty, Pat   20
Ellison, Ralph   30
Fadeaway   9, 14–15
Foster, Andrew Rube   4–9, 12, 14-16, 18-20, 22, 24-29, 32-38
Foster, Andrew, Sr.   7
Fowler, John "Bud"   23, 31
Gentlemen's Agreement   17
Great Depression   37
Hartsel, Topsy   16
Hill, Pete   20
Indianapolis ABCs   35
Johnson, Grant "Home Run"   20, 27, 31
Johnson, Walter   22
Kansas City Call   30
Kansas City Monarchs   36
Kansas City YMCA   32
Leland, Frank   19, 20

Leland Giants   19, 20
Lloyd, John Henry "Pop" 20-21, 27
Major League Baseball   16, 23, 31, 34-35, 38,
Malarcher, Dave   38
Mathewson, Christy   14-15
McGinnity, Iron Man   14-15
McGraw, John   14
Negro National League   6, 32-34, 37-38
Negro World Series   29
Newark Little Giants   17
Page Fence Giants   3, 31, 43
Petway, Bruce   27
Philadelphia Giants   10, 15-16, 18, 20
Powell, Willie   12
Price, Clement   32
Pullman railroad car   20, 31, 35
Raceball   20
Race Riot (1919)   29
Robinson, Jackie   23
Schorling, John   24
Schorling Park   24, 26
Screwball   9-10, 14, 20
Slavery   11, 23
Sol White's Baseball Guide   16
South Side Park   24
St. Louis Stars   37
Starkes, Charles   30
Stovey, George   17
Toledo Blue Stockings   23
Underground Railroad   23
Waco Yellow Jackets   8
Waddell, Rube   9
Wagner, Honus   15
Walker, Moses Fleetwood   17, 23
Watts, Sarah   20
White Sox   22, 24
Wickware, Frank   20
Wilkinson, J.L.   34
Williams, Joseph "Smokey Joe"   21–22
Young, Cy   27